MY PARENTING
Solutions

Positive Potty Training

THE NURTURING PARENT'S STEP-BY-STEP GUIDE

By Camilla McGill

Disclaimer: This book contains advice and information relating to childcare. It should be used as a supplement rather than replace the advice of your doctor or another trained health professional.

First Edition, Paperback and eBook, Kindle Direct Publishing 2022.

POSITIVE POTTY TRAINING -
THE NURTURING PARENT'S STEP-BY-STEP GUIDE

Printed by KDP Amazon
ISBN 978-1-3999-2023-0

Cover and book layout: Dominique Hazell
Photography: Adobe Stock Library

MY PARENTING
Solutions

Positive Potty Training

THE NURTURING PARENT'S STEP-BY-STEP GUIDE

By Camilla McGill

Table of Contents

DOWNLOAD RESOURCES

Scan this QR code to take you directly to the special page on my website where you can get a free download of some great resources that I refer to in the book.

- **Stop and Go signs to show children**
- **The My Parenting Solutions child-friendly anatomical diagram**
- **A booklet of resources of child-friendly potty training books, apps and songs**

Acknowledgements

Whilst writing this book, it's reminded me of the wonderful parents that I've reached around the globe who tell me that I've inspired and empowered them to respond to their children in a different and so much more nurturing way. They say they feel so much more confident as a result and hearing that reminds me of why I'm so passionate about my work.

I stay in touch with many of my clients and I hold them all close to my heart. Some, like Lisa Forsythe, went on one of my mini-video courses. Lisa wrote to me and said, "Your course on positive discipline was both reassuring and enlightening. I got some great ideas on ways to remain calm and to strengthen my boundaries with my toddler."

Many years ago I worked with Rachel Kelly (mother of 5). Rachel is a highly- respected and best-selling author and mental health advocate. When I sent Rachel my book, I was blown away by her summary of it so I thought I'd share it with you. "Camilla, I loved, loved, loved your book. Here's why it's so good. For a start, it is so attractively laid out and designed, matched by the ease and authority of the content. You give a real sense of who you're writing for - Parents who are really concerned about this key aspect of early childhood.

You are alongside us, the reader, the parent, not criticising or judging but encouraging and supporting. It's all in the gentle voice. Fascinating how potty training in miniature reflects so much of your philosophical wisdom and thoughts on parenting. Thanks for sharing it with me, Rachel"

I'd like to also acknowledge Tess Parsons-Broome who manages my marketing, and who has given me so much support and inspiration. Dominique Hazell, my hugely talented website and book designer who has always been so patient with my endless last-minute edits.

My four children helped inform so much of what I do and taught me so much about being a mother. They give me validation on what I do right and straight-talking feedback about what doesn't work, which is invaluable.

My husband Paul helps to run My Parenting Solutions and is endlessly encouraging and supportive of the work I do. There are so many things I couldn't do without him (even though I often forget to tell him this!).

I'd love to hear from you, do email me **camilla@myparentingsolutions.com** and tell me how you got on with the book. Also follow me on Instagram **@myparentingsolutions** to benefit from the tips I post on there.

Note from Camilla

I'm so glad you invested in my book. I'm Camilla McGill, I live in London and I'm a parent coach and a mother of four. I've worked with parents on every aspect of parenting for over 20 years and I'm passionate about helping parents make potty training a positive experience. I had some real challenges potty training my second child. Having discovered some great strategies for helping him, I started working with other parents. So, through extensive research, practical application and working with hundreds of parents, I've developed and refined a step by step, tried and tested guide to make potty training straightforward, simple and a really positive experience for both parents and children. I've also helped so many parents for whom this has gone wrong and I want to show you how to turn things around if you've had a bad experience.

INTRODUCTION

I want this book to give you confidence and trust in your own abilities as a parent or a caregiver. You really need to believe in yourself. I encourage parents with this all the time. Confidence will also come from being well-equipped and having the tools you're going to gain from this book. What makes potty training successful is preparing for the process rather than jumping in with an unrealistic expectation or comparing your child unfavourably with the miracle child who took one day to potty train and had no accidents! When you put in the time preparing, the process of actually getting your child dry and clean is so much smoother and quicker. By making potty training a smooth and successful process you'll also get to improve your connection and your communication with your child.

> ***"What I learned from Camilla's book went way beyond potty training. I knew I wanted to parent with empathy and compassion and it gave me the tools and validation to do that. I've learned how to help my child be cooperative by properly listening to her, putting her emotions into words and praising her descriptively."***
> Olivia, mother of a toddler

Getting to Know Your Child

Your child will give you lots of signals to show when they're ready, and in this book I show you how to look out for them. It's so important to understand your child and what motivates them. This will really help if you are one of the people reading this book who have started and failed at potty training. I show you how to work in partnership with your child and how to get your child involved to get them to **want** to be clean, to **want** to use the potty and to **want** to notice their body signals. I recommend you approach this stage in your child's life as an opportunity to get to know your child better and deepen your relationship with them.

> **"We had an unexpected bonus from using Camilla's techniques, not only did we nail potty training with our toddler but our older son has become so more confident with increased self esteem and has become really proud of his own achievements."**
> Fleur England, GP

When you use the skills of Descriptive Praise and validating your child's emotions using Reflective Listening (described in later chapters) you will without doubt deepen your relationship with your child taking it way beyond potty training which as a parent is absolutely invaluable. This will also be the case for your relationship with other children you have - even if they are well past potty training.

When you know your child better, you'll figure out what works for them. What works for another child may not work for your child. It may be that you have an older child whom you trained without any trouble, but you are facing problems with a second child. We need to remind ourselves that each child is different and will have different motivation and temperament to other children.

The final section in the book is dealing with setbacks and resistance. Inevitably there will be some children who have setbacks and there will be some children who may start off well but then become resistant to potty training or regress, so I cover all the tools and tips to deal with that.

“I’d witnessed a friend approaching potty training in a way I felt was pretty harsh, getting really cross with her child and telling her off for accidents. I knew I didn’t want to do it that way but I wanted guidance as I felt my child was ready. I loved Camilla’s approach. We didn’t rush at it, we got creative with it, and the whole process went so smoothly.”

Annette Williams

SECTION 1: GET READY

Now I suspect you'll want to just jump straight into the next stage, which is getting your child to remove their nappies and get on with potty training. However you need to invest some time getting ready in order to save you time and stress later on (even if you have started and it isn't going so well). Think of preparing for a trip, they always go smoother when you have done the prep! It may not take as long as you think, but just make sure that you go through these sections and if nothing else, they're going to give you some really good skills and ideas as a parent. Thorough preparation makes situations that could be challenging or stressful become so much easier. Please read this section even if you have started as there may well be something that you have missed that you can still address with your child.

GETTING YOURSELF PREPARED

If you've got a lot going on then you might want to delay the process or have a look at what you could say 'no' to and what you could cut back on. You need to be both psychologically and emotionally ready to tackle this process. You're going to be so well equipped that you're going to find it easier than you think. But nevertheless, if your life is really full or you are very distracted, then you're probably not ready to work with your child.

Can You Learn Patience?

I am not the most patient of people, but I've learned to develop it. It's something that I've really had to work on as a parent, and I use the tools of meditation and relaxation which I find really helpful. So if you don't feel like you're the most patient person either, find some ways to help develop it. Patience is also about managing your expectations and realising that children are different from us. Children are impulsive, they take time to adjust to change, they don't like transitions – moving from one thing to another abruptly - they are often fighting for control and sometimes they are rigid about what they do or don't want to do. Knowing these things are normal in children helps us to develop our patience.

Do You Have the Time?

We never ever have enough time in life, but ask yourself if you'd like to make potty training a priority as I promise it's worth it!

Should Day Care or Nursery Take the Lead?

Normally nurseries don't want to take total responsibility for this but are keen to work with parents and do the best for your child. I've covered some points in a later section.

Do You Know Your Child?

Parents usually know their children better than they realise. When you know what to look out for it makes it so much easier. It is also useful to ask anyone else involved in their care to give you their observations. Trust your own instinct the most though.

We thought we were ready to tackle potty training but our daughter was so fearful and unhappy. We were at a total loss to know what to do. Camilla's approach showed us how to stand in our daughter's shoes and figure out ways to help her feel confident and at ease with it. We listened to her and encouraged her and she proudly uses the potty now.

David Haines

FOCUS ON STAGE NOT AGE

Potty training is about **stage** not **age**. Children potty train at different ages. Maybe you have a friend who has a child of 18 months old and is potty trained and you're feeling like it's time for your child to potty train because your child is the same age. Remind yourself that children develop at different stages. If you think about this, when you were watching your child learn to crawl, I suspect that your child crawled or walked at a different age to other children. When your child was ready to walk you would have worked with him and encouraged him but if you pushed it too early, you wouldn't have achieved anything. So the normal age range to potty train is anything between 18 months (which in my view is VERY early) and 3½. If you approach it with confidence and engage your child, they are normally ready between the age of 2 and 3 years old. Some methods such as the Elimination Communication will teach you early potty training, which is a different approach to mine and usually more messy and time-consuming.

SIGNS OF READINESS:

There are lots of different ways to decide whether your child is ready and this book gives so many ways to engage them and motivate them but if ultimately you feel they aren't ready yet, then trust your instincts and wait.

1. A Dry Nappy

A dry nappy? Have you noticed that when you go to change a nappy, it's still dry? A good way of testing this is by using the kitchen paper towel test. Put a folded-up piece of kitchen paper towel in your child's nappy. After 60 - 90 minutes, test it and see if it's wet. I get you to do this because generally nappies are so absorbent that even if your child has done a small wee you wouldn't necessarily be able to tell. So if after an hour (or so), if it's still dry, it indicates that their bladder has the capacity to hold onto their urine for that length of time. Test this over a day because you may find that at one point, after half an hour it's wet, but later on the in day after 90 minutes it is still dry. So that will give you an indication if they have the ability to hold it for a decent length of time.

2. Predictable Bowel Movements

If you know that they poo at a fairly predictable time, perhaps after breakfast or after a meal, it will be helpful. Then you will be able to introduce the potty just before that bowel movement for them to see if they can do something into the potty. If their bowel movements aren't predictable, don't worry, you can still successfully potty train. It's worth keeping a note over 5-7 days of when they pooped as there may be more of a pattern than you think.

3. They Notice They Are Going to Wee

They notice and tell you they are going to do a wee or a poo. If they don't notice, it doesn't mean to say they aren't ready, this is just one of the signs. This doesn't mean to say you're going to leap straight in and whip the nappies off, but that is a sign that they're getting ready to potty train.

Also watch out for some non-verbal signals before they do a wee or poo, such as:

- They get a far-away look
- They stop talking and go quiet
- They move from one foot to another
- They let out little farts
- They move their hips around
- They wiggle their toes
- They put their hand to their bottom
- They touch their genital area
- Their breathing can speed up or slow down
- They look from side to side, moving their head

4. They Notice When They're Going to Do a Poo

Sometimes they might tell you beforehand that they're about to do a poo, or they might say nothing, but they disappear to a private place. It is extremely common for children to take themselves off to somewhere quiet in order to poo – and sometimes this continues even when they are wearing underwear. Hiding away shows that they do have body awareness to know when the poo is coming and your job will be to work with this. If they request a nappy to poo in once you've removed nappies then **don't** have a fight about it , give them a nappy and you'll figure out how to get them to poo straight in the potty or toilet. Later on in the book I deal with how to avoid the 'stealthy poo' in their underwear and avoid their need to poo in a nappy.

5. Clutching Their Bottom

Clutching onto their genital area or their bottom before they produce something. That's showing you, and it's probably unconscious for them at this moment, that they have a body awareness. That they are aware that something is going to come out or has just come out.

6. They Understand the Difference Between Wet & Dry

They understand the difference between wet and dry, clean and dirty and up and down. These concepts help when you start to talk to them about whether their underwear is wet or dry or whether their bottom is clean or dirty. Up and down is a good concept for pulling their pants up or down.

7. Showing Interest in You, Another child or Their Siblings Going to the Toilet

Showing interest in you, another child or their siblings going to the toilet. It indicates curiosity that you can build on. They might like helping to flush it or want to take a look at what has been produced. If your child is showing an interest in you or other people on the toilet, make sure that you leave the toilet door open when you're going, so they can come in and see what you're doing and talk about the process. They may have also seen other children on the toilet and you should definitely encourage it. They may like to practise sitting on the potty or toilet themselves, or they may be showing an interest in wearing underwear. Just watch your tone of voice as if you say, "Tom is using the potty" with a tone and a pitch that says, "So should you", they will feel pressured and we don't want that.

What Are Some Signs of Readiness?

They're able to communicate physical needs such as hunger, thirst or tiredness. Here's a pro-parenting tip which isn't related to potty training but I thought I'd throw it in anyway!. Children will often be very demanding about hunger or thirst. And as a parent you can coach them into being more polite and well mannered. So whilst they probably bark at you, "I'm hungry." You can step in here and ask them to make a request. You could say, "What do you want to ask me for?" More examples could be: "Make me a sandwich." To which you reply, "I'm happy to make you a sandwich but first you need to say, "Please, may I have a sandwich?'"

Or they might tell you, "I'm thirsty", and you say to your child, "Are you asking for a drink of water? Then you need to ask me nicely, "Please, may I have some water?".

So it's a good policy, when you can, to have them make requests rather than barking orders at you. We don't want to be seen as their slave, even though we will very frequently feel that way.

They may show another physical need of tiredness by being irritable or rubbing their eyes if they're tired or even asking to go to bed. Asking to go to bed might seem extraordinary to some of you, but I know it is possible as my third child, Scarlett, used to ask to go to bed! How we loved that request!

Lastly, a good sign that your child is ready for potty training is that they've got good general gross motor skills, so they can run, maybe they can hop and they can jump with two feet. These are signs that they've got the awareness and the physical capacity to deal with the mechanics of using a potty or a toilet.

GETTING YOUR CHILD READY

This next stage can take a good few weeks or a very short time depending on the stage your child is at when you start. Practice makes perfect. The more you practise with them, the easier it's going to be. Practising things like washing their hands, sitting on a potty, taking their clothes on and off. All these things really help make it much easier to transition when it comes to removing their nappy. If you are reading this book having had an unsuccessful attempt already, then I suggest you go back to practising, without any pressure that they actually wee or poo on the potty.

1. Picking Out Nice Underwear in Preparation

This can be a real motivator for some children but don't expect it's the only thing you need to do! Pick something with their favourite character or colour. Underwear with the days of the week is fun, although parents have reported dramas when it's Tuesday and they can't find 'Tuesday' pants'. Go to a shop and pick them or have a look online, but it needs to be something they like the look of, not just you picking it out.

2. Picking Out a Potty

Depending on your child, their size and agility combined with their preference, you might decide to start with a potty (or potty chair as they call it in America). If you opt for the toilet, then a toilet seat insert is pretty important. This needs to be very stable with something that stops it wobbling and make sure you have a step so they can get up to the toilet easily.

I do recommend starting with a potty because you can keep them close to your child and have more than one, plus it's a better sitting position for poo. But whether you go for potty or toilet seat, I suggest you make sure you get a good fit. If you can, choose a colour that appeals to your child or find one with a character (but don't be swayed to buy one with a character if it isn't a good fit). Quality is important here because if you've picked out a cheap one that could easily tip over, it might cause them to be fearful or uncomfortable and resist using it. I happen to like Baby Bjorn, as I think they are ergonomically well designed for children.Some parents buy those little toilets that make a flushing sound. Whatever you buy, make sure it fits their shape nicely.

3. Process of Elimination and Learning How Their Body Works

Start to talk to your child about the process of elimination. What do I mean by that? I mean what happens to food and drink when it goes through your body. Explain that when they drink, that gets turned into wee. That the liquid is used by their body to hydrate and the rest of it comes out as wee. Same with food. The food that they eat gives them energy and helps them grow and the waste stuff turns into poo. Talk about how their body is working; their muscles are used to make them run, jump and climb, their eyes let them see. Their digestive system takes all the food and uses it for their body and the waste stuff - wee and poo - is what they don't need. When they understand all those functions of their body, they feel proud of themselves. See the anatomical diagram and the chapter on Superscience for more on this.

POTTY TRAINING ACCORDING TO YOUR CHILD'S TEMPERAMENT

I wonder if you've thought about what kind of temperament and personality type your child has? They may actually have a mixture of more than one type, but anyone who's been around children at all will be able to see that children are all so different and they have different temperaments and personality types. I've listed the most common types below to help you identify your child and see how you can adapt your approach accordingly.

Persistent and Strong-willed

If you have a persistent and strong-willed child, it can feel that they are quite a challenge and you may need a little bit of extra patience with them around potty training. These children like to make their own choices and they may be prone to emotional outbursts when they can't do what they want. They respond well when you validate their emotions. You'll get loads of examples of that in the reflective listening section. It may be that you, as a parent, need to really work on your own stress levels because these types of children can be a bit of a handful.

Sensitive

This type of child can be very sensitive to smells and touch. They may react to the sensation of things, like the feel of the potty or the toilet seat. That's why with these children you need to make sure that whatever you buy is a good fit because if that potty tips, it can put them off, if the toilet seat insert slips, that can give them a fright as they may fear falling in. They need time to adapt to these things. They may also be sensitive to the sounds of the flush of the toilet or using a toilet or potty in different environments. Make sure the potty is in a place which is the right temperature for them, some like warmth, some like it to be cooler. So we need to make the process very calm and physically comfortable for them.

Distractible and Impulsive

Most children are distracible and impulsive, but highly distractible and impulsive kids notice everything that's going on around them and they can be very easily distracted from the task in hand. So when it comes to them needing to sit on a potty, it can be quite difficult because they don't want to sit around or wait. With this type of child, with a high activity level, start off with an expectation that they're going to have a short period sitting. We need to make it fun for them as they can get bored easily and ideally have the potty in a place without too much else going on or they'll get very distracted! It will help to keep a few things around to engage them, whether it's songs or a busy bag to keep next to the potty that has stuff in it that they like and enjoy.

Adaptable or Difficulty with Adapting

Some children adapt very easily and they'll probably take to the idea of using the potty quite quickly. Others will find it hard to adapt to a change. They may be the type of child who finds it hard to adapt to changes in routine or environment. These kids may need plenty of time to practise their skills and lots of praise and encouragement for the very small steps of progress that they make. They may need some extra help adjusting to using a potty away from home. They may also resist going without a nappy because they've become so used to it.

Extrovert

This type of child loves involvement. They're excited around people and they probably won't mind sitting on a potty with others around them. They may not mind being in a toilet outside of their home environment. They may enjoy the performance of using the potty and want you to be there and watch and they may not respond well to being left alone.

Introvert

An introvert takes time to reflect and take their time over things. They may keep themselves to themselves a little bit. They like their own company and they may prefer privacy on a potty or a toilet. They probably wouldn't like it if the potty is in a main room or in an environment where there are too many other people around.

Now, there will be overlaps between these temperament types. Your child won't neatly fit into one, but it's just useful to know what kind of things to be aware of which will help you and your child adapt.

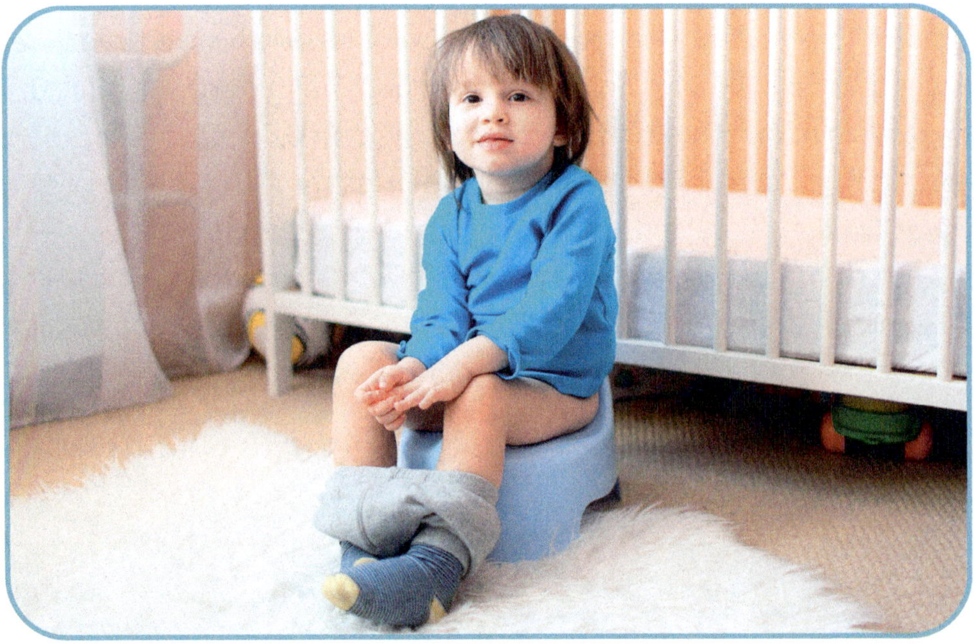

PSYCHOLOGICAL PREPARATION

I suspect the idea of doing 'psychological preparation' for potty training would be scoffed at by sceptics of modern parenting ideology, however, there is so much research now on how damaging potty training can be if it isn't handled gently. The fact is, our emotions are inextricably linked to our physiology, and we all know how our digestive system can go haywire under stress don't we?

Some children will be excited about getting the next step, taking away their nappies, and others will need help adjusting to the idea. Even those who are excited about it, might find that the reality isn't as fun or as easy as they imagined. Saying goodbye to their nappies can be hard and they can be reticent about losing them. So one of the ways to psychologically prepare a child is to put into words what you think they're feeling. There is more about this in the section on validating emotions, but to give you an example you might say, **"You like your nappy. It feels safe to you and you are used to wearing it".**

Or, **"When you take off your nappy, it's a strange feeling to be naked".**

If a child has been naked and felt wee trickling down their legs you might say, **"It's a funny feeling when wee runs down your legs. Maybe it feels cold and you aren't used to it".**

For those children who are excited about the idea of leaving nappies behind, you can reflect on that and say, **"Isn't it going to be fun that you don't have to have nappies anymore and you can take yourself to the toilet? You're going to be so grown up and you'll be wearing your new underwear!".**

I would suggest you are aware that they may have both feelings, a mixture of excitement and apprehension. Talk to them about how today they can do so much for themselves and they're becoming so much more independent in so many ways. It's great to communicate the idea of progress and talk to them about how far they've progressed and get them feeling excited about the idea of potty training being a part of progression.

PREPARING FOR TOILET ROUTINES

Talk about the different times of day when children use the potty. They probably follow you into the toilet so talk to them about when you need to use the toilet. Describe the different times of the day for regular visits to the potty or toilet: when they first wake up in the morning, before they go out, before (or after) each meal, before bath time and before bedtime. Young kids would probably make more potty visits than this but if you explain routine visits and even do pretend-play about it, they'll be mentally prepared.

Talk to them about the fact that when they first go without a nappy, they're probably going to need to go more frequently than you do because their bladder capacity is growing and it doesn't hold as much as a grown up. You might be thinking, "How would my 2 year old understand that concept?". Well, the younger the child, the more you'll need to simplify your language but you can gesture and use the **Balloon Experiment on page 61.**

Bladder Capacity

Most parents, and certainly most children, don't really realise this, but the bladder capacity for a child between 2 and 3 years old is approimately 180ml, which is about 6oz. On **page 11** you'll see a great experiment to do with your child that shows them what their bladder capacity is.

Nappy Free Time

It's good to practice help kids take their clothing off, and encouraging them to sit on the potty so they have practice times without a nappy. This can be great before their bath in the evening, or if the weather is warm or your house is well-heated you can do it at other times of the day. Take off their nappy, so they can run around without one and do sitting practice without an expectation that they'll actually produce a wee or poo.. You may well at that point be able to catch them and get them to produce something on the potty or on the toilet but don't have that as a goal to start with.

The Outside World

Depending on what stage you're at, at this point, they may be able to get the concept that when they go out, you're going to take a travel potty with you or that you'll find toilets for them to use. When you go out, take them to the toilet with you and explain that kids and adults use toilets (or travel potties) when they leave the house. Discuss with your child the transition to their nursery or day care. Find out who's going to help them at the nursery. Visit the toilet there so that they're psychologically prepared in advance. All this is going to help you make fast progress. There's more about transition to the outside world on **page 77**.

FOMO and 'Stop' and 'Go'

Kids will need to interrupt play to use the potty which they find irritating and they often get FOMO. In case you didn't know, FOMO is Fear Of Missing Out and it's a big feature with children. Quite often when children have an accident it is because they're so intent on doing what they're doing they just don't notice their body signals. They may know they need to go but worry that if they interrupt an activity to use the potty, they may not be able to come back to it, so they ignore the signals and have an accident. It doesn't mean that they are lazy or defiant, it means they don't want to stop doing what they are doing.

Therefore, you need to talk to them about the fact that they need to stop, go and use the potty, and then they can come back. Reassure them that they'll be able to come back to what they're doing. If you know that the activity is actually over - say for example, it's time to leave the house, you can put the game aside for later or validate that it is hard to stop doing what you love. You can download these 'Stop' and 'Go' signs from the My Parenting Solutions - **www.myparentingsolutions.com/pottyresources.**

PARTNERSHIP WITH OTHER ADULTS

Now it's time to start thinking about other people involved in your childcare. Who else has interactions with your child? Do they spend a consistent amount of time with a grandparent? Do they go to a child-minder? If you're separated, do they have time with the other parent? All those people involved in your childcare need to be part of the potty training process and ideally using the same terminology, particularly regarding the words you use for poo, wee, penis, vagina, toilet, loo, bathroom. Whatever words you choose, it is better if everyone is consistent. Or it may be that you just need to adapt your child to the fact that at their nursery or grandma, use different terminology. Check out the other environments and the attitude of the other people. What you really want is for everyone to be on the same page. You want everybody to have a positive attitude. You want the environment to be calm and friendly towards your child's potty training.

Good partnerships (with anyone else involved in the care of your child) are going to be what helps make potty training successful. Good communication, making sure that when things start to get moving with potty training, you're communicating with each other and you're telling each other what is working and what isn't working. But if things aren't going so well, don't discuss this within your child's earshot or they will start to develop shame and embarrassment which you do NOT want.

Case Study

Parveen came to me in distress with her son Ahmed (aged 3 ¾). His potty training just wasn't progressing and he was having frequent accidents at his pre-school. She told me that the teachers handed her the soiled clothes at the end of the day. not only in front of Ahmed, but also within earshot of other parents and children. She said she had a knot in her stomach every time she collected him. They told her how many accidents he'd had and in a fairly critical tone would turn to Ahmed and say, "We can't keep disrupting everything to change you. You must tell us when you need the toilet". Now you might think that would motivate Ahmed to do better, but it didn't. It made him anxious and far more likely to have an accident. I advised Parveen to meet the teacher to request that nothing was discussed in front of Ahmed. At the same time, she and her husband taught him about how his body worked and made fun games about his brain:body connection (more about this later). They stopped nagging him about going to the toilet and taught him how to trust himself to notice. Within a few weeks, he had gained so much confidence and was barely having an accident at school and if he did, it was dealt with much more discreetly.

SHOPPING LIST

So here are items for you to go shopping for or to borrow. And I'm not suggesting spending too much money, but just make sure you're prepared.

Pants / Knickers / Underwear - Use Whatever Term Works for You

First thing on the list would be underwear. I mentioned this already, but special underwear picked out by your child can be motivating to them. It could be a special character. It could be a colour. It could be a design that they like. Make sure that your child likes the underwear but keep it to one side until they stop wearing nappies.

Toilet Seat Inset or Potty and Step

Make sure that it's a good quality one that fits their size and their shape and that your child finds it appealing. The toilet seat insert shouldn't slip around if you're using one of those. A step is a necessity, for climbing up to the toilet and for standing on to wash their hands.

Photography: Baby Bjorn

Potty Friendly Clothing

You want to have clothes that are easy to pull up and pull down, so you don't want clothes that are tight with buttons, zips or any complicated fasteners. You also want to make sure you've got plenty of clothes, things like leggings, sweatpants, shorts with elasticated waists, wide skirts or dresses that they can easily lift up to sit down. I'm a big believer in protecting the planet as much as we can so try second-hand children's clothes shops for potty friendly clothing.

Pull-ups and Trainer Pants

I don't advise either of these once you've removed their nappies. Pull-ups can be used prior to 'going for it' for your child to get used to pulling them up and down but after that, I don't advise them. Both pull-ups and trainer pants are highly absorbent and will take away the sensation we want them to have when they need to go. By all means continue to use pull-ups for night time (night time training, in my opinion, comes a minimum of 6 months after daytime training, unless you have a child with a particularly strong, mature bladder). If your child is still napping, you'll probably need to continue with a pull up or nappy for a while as they are unlikely to hold it in during their sleep.

Taking Precautions for the Mess

Are you the sort of person who is worried about the mess on the carpets or soft-furnishings and has been delaying potty training because you feel anxious? I'm not judging here. Everyone has different levels of tolerance. I expect you had no idea before you had children how much more tolerant you'd be of dealing with mess. My advice would be to take certain precautions but also work on 'letting it go'. Urine is sterile and poo-mess (although unpleasant to clear up) will come out with some soapy water. Getting rid of those nappies and helping your child become potty trained really needs to be more of a priority than protecting the carpets - but I do get that it's harder for some parents than others to tolerate it. Also known as piddle pads, for the buggy and the car seat can be useful.

Protector Pads

Be prepared that there will be some mess and **old towels** are good for cleaning it up. You might also want an **old blanket** for putting over the sofa for watching TV, as they may not notice they've wet themselves.

Busy Bag

What's a busy bag? I hear you ask. This can be a basket or a cloth bag and your child picks out some of their favourite toys and books to putin it. You make a rule that the busy bag stays next to the potty and you give it to your child once they've sat down. If they run off, the bag and contents go away again. Putting it away is never presented as a punishment, it's simply that the bag and potty go together. You'll find that you need to rotate what's in it to keep them interested and motivated to look inside the bag. You can even hide small objects in there and they can search inside with their eyes closed and guess what the object is.

SECTION 2: WORKING TOGETHER

This section covers **working in partnership with your child** and with your support network. It really helps to establish a partnership before you remove a nappy. I can't say how long you need to spend on this section. It may be not long at all or maybe you'll need to put a little bit more time into this process.

CREATING A PARTNERSHIP WITH MY CHILD

I'm very keen on nurturing the partnership between you and your child. This isn't just for now, but for the future too. You'll find it so helpful for effective, calm and collaborative parenting. The idea of working in partnership and the principle and practice of working in partnership does wonders to strengthen your relationship.

So first and foremost, stay confident and keep calm yourself. If you need some support, listen to a relaxation audio, learn meditation, talk to a good friend, use supportive mums or dads networks or lean on non-judgemental members of your family. Staying confident is about trusting your own abilities as a parent and also using the tools that you're learning.

You might see some of the signs we mentioned in the previous section that your child is ready to start potty training, such as unconsciously touching

their genitals or their bottom. You might have noticed facial signals etc. These signs are your child's way of communicating with you. You will be able to use descriptive praise and reflective listening to help move this communication forward. You want your child to feel comfortable. Sometimes we can frown, tut, be a little brusque without realising.

If your child has had accidents we can show our frustration with a sigh. If they've got a big steaming poo in their pants or nappy we can wrinkle up our nose. All of this comes across to your child as judgement and disapproval and will dent our connection with them and their willingness to cooperate with us.

MOTIVATING YOUR CHILD

Descriptive praise, which is covered later in this section, is the most important and most powerful motivator and I recommend that you start using it straight away with your child. It takes time to practice using it as it is like learning a new language. Some children are motivated by things like stickers and reward charts. I'm not a fan of reward charts in order to get your child to produce something on the potty.

The aim is that they are noticing and acting on their body signals, in order to have a good feeling of doing a wee or a poo not in order to get a sticker or reward. In the long term this is much more effective. Children can be motivated by other things; perhaps to read a certain book or play with a doll while they have some sitting time. Sometimes you can use a monitoring chart that's like a little checklist, this isn't a sticker chart to get rewards, it's just a tick or sticker chart to monitor when they've sat on the potty even if they don't produce anything. It rewards cooperation which is important.

It's also really vital that you use descriptive praise (in the next section), not just for potty training but for all areas of child rearing. Use it with any other children you have as well. Learning descriptive praise is a gift to your child. Also in the next section is how to recognise what your children's emotions are and how to validate them. This helps your child to understand that emotions are driving their behaviour. This is another fantastic gift for you because it's just so important to help your child be emotionally balanced and grounded and help them to deal with issues like fears or frustrations in a nurturing way.

SUPER SCIENCE, ANATOMY AND PHYSIOLOGY

In this section I explain what's physiologically happening with your child. We're covering the science behind the creation of wee and poo and also understanding anatomy and physiology and teaching your child. You can explain all this to them in a way that they find fascinating. Children are often really curious about the science side of potty training and learning about their anatomy, it's a great way to hook them and get them motivated. When you study and understand it yourself, it makes it much easier to explain it to your child.

Case Study

Jasmine and Keyan came to me about their daughter Lianna aged 3½ who had developed a huge fear of weeing on the potty or toilet. They'd tried everything - rewards of sweets and stickers, then bigger and what they felt would be more tempting rewards. It made no impact on Lianna at all. She'd do anything to avoid using the potty. Jasmine had offered to keep her in nappies all day but Lianna didn't want that either. Jasmine and Keyan weren't bad parents and what Lianna was experiencing wasn't unusual. They started to talk to Lianna about how amazing her body was. They showed her the anatomical diagram shown below and got her to point to her body parts. They made up a wee song together and encouraged her to come to the toilet with them as much as possible. They explained how her brain was so amazing at telling her bladder muscles that they can relax and let the wee out and validated Lianna's fears about letting go. Within a couple of weeks Lianna was barely having an accident and was happily using the toilet without fear.

THE PHYSICAL PROCESS

Children love anything scientific and getting them to understand the science behind their bodies and the brain-body connection is often what makes the biggest difference with successful, smooth, trouble-free potty training.

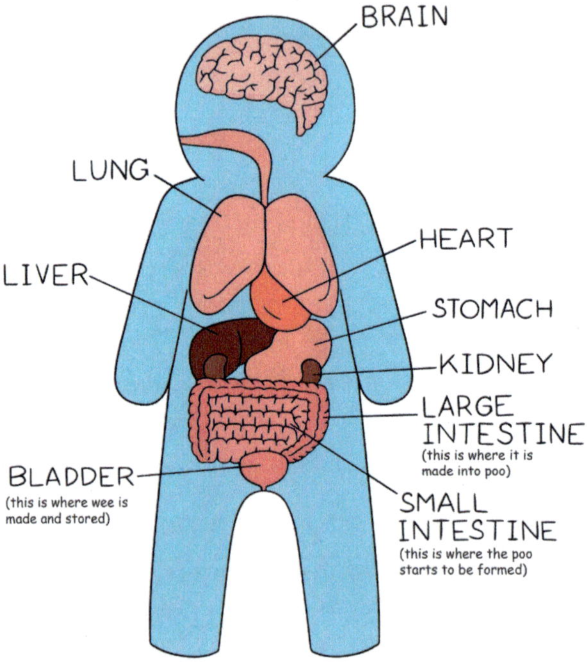

I don't suppose you've thought much about how wee is made have you? It's actually really fascinating and people rarely talk about this to their children, probably because few of us know the science.

Urine is formed in the kidneys from the fluid we drink, it's composed of excess water waste and a product called urea. It then passes from the kidneys and into the bladder. The bladder is a hollow, muscular organ and it stretches. It sits at the base of the pelvis. For a child between the age of 2 and 3 1/2, it will hold approximately 180ml or 6floz. As a child gets older, it holds greater capacity. Urine leaves the bladder via the urethra; a muscular tube and the external sphincter is voluntarily controlled by the body's central nervous system. The brain is capable of receiving messages from and sending messages to the bladder. And this is where the whole mind-body connection starts to get really interesting because as they get older the brain gets more capable of receiving the message.

Teaching your child about the connection between the brain and the bladder is going to engage your child in this process and help them understand what's going on. Talk to them about how wee is made and the messages that their brain is sending. You can even tell them that the connection is linked to our emotions. The happier and the more relaxed the child is, the better the connection they will have between their body and their brain. If they are under stress or pressure, then the connections are different. So that's why a child under stress may well wet themselves or they may have a sudden bowel movement. They can also do the opposite and hold on to it for fear of letting go.

So, when you talk about wee and poo, you want to make the separation between the brain and body. For wee say things like, **"Is your bladder telling your brain that it needs a wee?".** Also when they sit on a potty you say, **"Does your brain need to tell your bladder to relax to let the wee out?".** As you use the words, point to your head and your abdomen as you describe the brain and the body area. You can simplify it to using 'tummy' instead of 'bladder and bowel' if you want to make it easier but, the more language you use, the quicker they grasp what you mean.

"The muscles in your bowel give signals to your brain and when the poo needs to come out, the muscles push it out. You can tell your muscles to push when you sit on the potty".

“You can also tell the muscles in your bladder or in your bottom to hold on until you reach the potty so you make it in time”.

As adults if we’re particularly stressed, we might have loose bowels or desperately need to go to the loo. Children experience stress and anxiety in the same way. What might seem like nothing to us, might make them feel anxious - things like the flush of a toilet or if we have overreacted to an accident at one point. The diagram, which is included again on this page, gives you a good visual to show your child about the mind-body connection.

You can download this Body Diagram and use for discussion from My Parenting Solutions: **www.myparentingsolutions.com/pottyresources.**

Explain to your child how amazing their body is and that their brain gives messages to their bladder and bowel to tell them they need to go to the toilet.

Other things you can explain to them is that their lungs help them breathe. Their heart pumps blood around their body. The liver that takes out any toxins. Show them the mouth, where food first goes and gets chewed and goes into the stomach and then into the small intestine, which is where the food starts to be formed into poo. The nutrients are taken out and the large intestine is where food is made into poo. Poo is all the waste bits that the body doesn’t need. The large intestine is also called the colon or bowel and muscles in the colon push the poo down. After that it gets pushed out by the bottom (sphincter) muscles which respond to signals from their brain which tells the muscles to push.

Water also gets swallowed by the mouth, it gets filtered by the kidneys, it hydrates the body (in the same way water hydrates a plant) and it eventually reaches the bladder where it is stored as wee (or urine).

You will want to simplify some of this depending on your child's capacity to understand, but it's handy to know.

Poo is something that their body has produced and it's very easy to make nasty faces and comments about the smell that they've made. Much better to approach it with admiration and respect which will help them feel good about the whole process. And feeling good about the whole process is one of the real keys to making it successful, for them to feel that you're on their side, that you are showing them love and respect for what they've made.

INCREASE YOUR CHILD'S CONFIDENCE AND MOTIVATION USING DESCRIPTIVE PRAISE

Descriptive praise is going to transform your parenting. Make sure that you really study it and learn the words of descriptive praise, you will find it has such a positive impact on your child for potty training and beyond. Using praise and encouragement is a powerful, easy way to motivate children, you probably know that and I'm sure you praise your kids. However we tend to praise evaluatively. "Good boy.", "Well done.", "Good girl.", "Fantastic." This doesn't have the same impact it would if it was descriptive. What do I mean by descriptive? You add value to your praise by adding information, rather than just telling them generally they are a "Good boy/ good girl" or the superlatives like 'You are amazing', these don't have anything like the same impact as when you praise descriptively.

Here are Some Examples of Descriptive Praise:

"You stretched up high to reach your teddy and you didn't even have to get my help".

"You took off your own coat and hung it up on the peg. That's very independent."

What we would normally say if we saw a child do something like hanging up a coat would be, "great, well done." But we didn't give them the information about exactly what it is that they did. This information allows them to replicate what it is that you're noticing. Instead say, **"You know that we hang our coat on the peg instead of dropping it on the floor and you took yours off and put it in exactly the right place. That is very cooperative!".**

We want to start linking praise to the potty. **"You were playing just now but when I said, 'Let's use the potty', you said, 'Ok' and you came straight away! You didn't make a wee yet but that's ok, you are still making progress!".**

We need to praise the process and all the small steps in the right direction. Don't wait for the end result. When it's related to the potty, don't wait for them to actually produce a wee.

You can say, **"You interrupted your game and you came to sit on the potty, that was so independent of you".**

As you see you are adding the quality that you're seeing – in this instance being 'independent'. Independence is key. When we link the quality with the steps that they took, they start to get a really positive perception of themselves.

"You can feel proud that you sat on the potty, even though at first you said you didn't want to try. Now look at that amazing poo that you made, your muscles pushed it out!".

It's important for your child to have an intrinsic sense of self. When you say, **"You can feel proud of yourself"**, that's giving your child an internal pride, rather than you feeling proud of them. It's also nice that they know you feel proud of them, but more importantly they should feel proud of themselves. Don't wait for them to have done something amazing.

Praise all the small steps, the little things that they're doing. By doing this you're connecting with them, with what they're doing and you're motivating them to want to replicate it. The term 'You get more of what you focus on' is so true with kids. If we focus on the things we don't want them to do and tell them off, they will inevitably do more of that, so we want to **'Catch the good'**. Also don't forget to use an enthusiastic tone of voice with little children.

"I had bought everything possible - potties, trainer pants, pants, reward stickers etc - but I just didn't know where to start and was slightly dreading the whole process! This approach was just what I needed to give me the confidence to take the next step. I realised that we weren't quite ready and needed to spend a bit more time preparing our son. I'm so pleased we waited because our little boy (aged 2 ½) nailed potty training in a few days once we got him ready!"
Harriet Wood

Let's look at praising the progress.

"You can pull your pants down all by yourself. I used to have to help you but now you have done it for yourself!".

"You used to say 'no' when I asked you to try and now you said, 'okay Daddy'".

"You used your muscles to hold in the wee/poo until you reached the potty. Now your underwear is still dry!".

I'm using here the examples related to the toilet, but you can use this praise for progress on all fronts. Maybe your child has stopped asking you for a bottle a night, so you can praise for progress with that.

Other examples are things such as, **"You're becoming so grown up today you did four wees on the potty, and yesterday it was only two".**

"You helped mummy when you pulled off the toilet paper for me, that was kind".

We're wanting to develop good character traits such as kindness and helpfulness and we want to help them see themselves as capable. So we praise them for being generous, being kind, for sharing and for things like listening and following instructions. The more you mention it, the more they'll do. You get more of what you notice. And the same applies for the negative. You get more of what you focus on. That is how the brain works.

It's our job as parents to help them grow into confident children who are cooperative and want to please. And when we build our muscle of being able to use the language of descriptive praise, it has such an amazingly positive impact on our children.

Descriptive Praise Won't Come Naturally to Us

We have to learn to use descriptive praise, it won't roll off the tongue and it feels clumsy at first. It helps children's self-belief and their belief in their abilities. It goes hand in hand with a collaborative approach to parenting and potty training. It feels like you're on the same team if you're praising them a lot. The rule should be ten praises for every one negative. Try it out. It isn't easy at first, but it gets easier the more you do it and you'll feel like a much better parent when you praise your child.

HELP YOUR CHILD TO ADAPT EMOTIONALLY

How Do Children's Emotions Impact Upon Potty Training?

Anyone who's been around a toddler will know that they're absolutely full of emotions. They will change from being ecstatically happy to angry or sobbing and sad in the space of a few seconds. Our job is to help them cope with their emotions. To do that we need to validate all their emotions. All their emotions are valid, even if they're emotions that we don't like, like jealousy or anger.

Don't diminish the emotions by saying things like, "Don't be silly, don't make a fuss or don't be sad". They're real and they're valid emotions. If you diminish or negate a child's emotion, it leaves them feeling that they're wrong or silly to be feeling a certain way. We need to help them to understand what their feelings are, and be ok with how they are feeling. I want you to take on board validating your child's emotions both with potty training and with every emotion they experience.

"I really wanted to say thank you for putting me at ease and for your positive approach to potty training. I'm feeling much more confident now. We're on day 3 with potty training and Seb smashed it. Thank you so much for this approach, not just on potty training but on sooo many things, it's all been so helpful as it fits right in with being the sort of mum I want to be."

Caryn McMullen

Examples of Emotions with Potty Training

- They might experience fear around not getting it 'right' and making mistakes
- Shame that they have wet or soiled themselves
- Anxiety about getting to the potty on time
- Disappointment that they can't trust their body yet
- Frustration they have to interrupt play
- Irritation if we ask them too much whether they need to go
- Fear of letting out a wee or a poo
- Wanting to have control in a world where they feel they are told what to do all the time

Not all children have an emotional response like this but many do. Frustration is a common emotion associated with potty training - both for us and our children!

They might feel frustrated having to sit and produce something on the potty or frustrated with themselves that nothing came out. They may express frustration with you for 'interrupting' their game or programme to have a try and they may show it by shouting, "I don't need the potty" when they clearly do as observed by their body language (particularly the potty jiggle). So we need to express these feelings for them. Asking how a toddler is feeling will rarely get the response you are looking for, but putting into words what you think they are feeling is very productive to help lower their resistance and give your child vocabulary for what they are feeling. More of this below in the **Reflective Listening** section.

Case Study

Freddie's mum, Lara, identified that he had a distractible, impulsive temperament. He would refuse to use the potty even though she knew he needed to and then five minutes later he'd wet himself. She'd start off dealing with it calmly, but by the 5th accident of the day, she was getting more and more cross with him, telling him off and making threats like 'if you don't use the potty when I ask, then you can't watch TV'. She told me she was becoming the sort of parent she really didn't want to be and was miserable about it so she started to use a different approach and praised him for all the little things she loved about him - his enthusiasm and high energy. She praised the fact he noticed so many things (he loved insects and would spot them in the garden and call her over to show her). He wasn't always impulsive and could sometimes stop before he grabbed his baby sister's rattle, for example. So she started to praise him for using self-control. Freddie blossomed as their connection grew stronger and he started to see himself in a better light. Lara decided to use Freddie's high energy to her advantage and did some competitions with him running to the bathroom together to see who could do a wee first. She also taught him how to listen to his body's signals more and used funny voices for his bladder speaking to his brain. It didn't take long for Freddie to barely have an accident.

If a child is resisting using the potty, just the recognition itself can help the feeling to shift.

"You don't like to stop your game and come to the potty. That feels boring", or, "You like to quietly poo in your pants, that's why you go behind the sofa to poo. Pooing in the potty doesn't feel so safe".

Now it might seem really strange to you to validate exactly what you DON'T want your child to do. What you are doing here is simply acknowledging your child's emotions and preferences, which helps them to feel that they are ok.

Once the emotion is validated, they are able to rationalise what they need to do or follow the instruction you are giving. Don't try to achieve co-operation via threats and criticism. It might work in the short term but in the long term it's destructive. Consistently using threats and criticism with a child will erode your relationship with them. It lowers trust, undermines your authority and reduces their self-esteem. Think longer term rather than quick fix. Invest time to learn descriptive praise and validating your child's emotions and you will be far more successful in getting your child to be cooperative, confident, motivated and communicative.

"Validating my child's emotions works like witchcraft when he's resistant. I used to resort to using threats and then not only would I feel bad, but my child quickly learnt I rarely follow through on them. Instead I now simply say things like 'I can see you are feeling frustrated. I know it's boring to stop playing and come to the potty'. He looks at me and 'bingo', he cooperates!"

Daisy Morris

VALIDATING CHILDREN'S EMOTIONS USING REFLECTIVE LISTENING

Reflective listening is the skill where you validate - i.e. put your child's feelings into words for them. If you ask a child, "Why did you wet yourself?", they will very rarely be able to tell you. They'll say, "I don't know", or "Because I did". If you ask what they are afraid of they'll give you a blank stare, shrug or say, "The cat" (when you know they love the cat!). But if you take a guess and put the emotions into words for them, it shows that you've understood them, that you're empathic and you're on their side. Having an accident is so annoying. When you're moving on to the stage when you've removed your child's nappy, they will have accidents and they might be frustrated by it - so will you, but as parents we have to keep that to ourselves! You're going to show empathy. Even if they don't appear to be in the slightest bit bothered by having an accident, at some level they will be feeling frustrated, so say things like:

"Having an accident feels annoying, it feels better if you make it to the potty doesn't it?".

It can be frustrating for children to have to have help pulling down their underwear. So you can reflect that by saying, **"It's so frustrating when you need help to get your underwear off"**, rather than, "Don't make a fuss", or "I've got to help and that's that!".

If they've sat on the potty and nothing came out you can say, **"You sat for a while and nothing came out. That feels like a waste of time".** In the early stages, or even later on, when they sit there and nothing is produced, they may feel frustrated by that. If you put that into words for them and acknowledge the frustration, it's going to help them deal with it so much quicker.

Communicate that this is a big stage for them. Sometimes change feels strange. Your child may be feeling unsettled about learning this new (and complicated) skill.

Let's face it, a nappy is easier for them and they've been wearing their nappies for a long time. We can show that we understand that they might not feel like growing up. So if they say, "I don't want to wear pants, I want my nappy back", you might say, **"Maybe you don't feel like being a grown up boy at the moment"**, or **"I understand how you must feel. Nappies are easier and that is what you are used to".**

You don't have to justify or explain anything. Just acknowledge it and acknowledge the resistance. **"It's annoying to have to stop what you're doing and come to the potty."** Or, **"You don't like it when you feel I rush you to do something on the potty".**

When you acknowledge resistance, rather than meeting them head on, it really helps to reduce the resistance. It lowers the resistance for them because they feel that you're on their team or on their side.

You could describe their confusion, "Maybe you aren't sure if your body is giving you a signal or not". That could be confusing for a child. They don't quite know when to trust themselves. Sometimes they've thought they needed a poo and they go and sit on the toilet and nothing comes which would feel disappointing or confusing.

"Our daughter regressed badly with potty training, she was fine at first but then had so many accidents and refused to use the potty when we asked her. So we turned to Camilla. We were amazed that the first few days after using Camilla's approach, Rosie had no accidents. We used the body picture, the monitoring chart and a lot of descriptive praise and we validated her emotions. In the first few weeks we had some days with one accident but many more with no accidents at all. Rosie not only went to the toilet when we asked her to try, but also told us when she needed to go and even held it in if we were out and needed to find a toilet. We couldn't believe we could have such success so quickly. We're so grateful to have found this approach as it really fits with our approach to parenting."

Nicola and Tom

PHRASES THAT VALIDATE EMOTIONS

"For you to push the potty away like that and shout "go away" shows me you're really frustrated. Maybe it isn't even about the potty and you're cross about something else".

For a lot of children, they don't like going without nappies as it means they don't have to stop what they're doing to go to the bathroom. Some will pretend that they haven't wet their underwear or pooed in it because they feel worried about your reaction. They may feel shame that they have done it or frustrated that this will mean they have to be cleaned up.

So say something like, **"When you told me that you hadn't done a poo, but you actually had, I think you felt worried that I would be cross"**, or, **"I think you felt embarrassed."** This is a very common occurrence for children. They will deny what they've done if they think you seem cross or they're worried about you having a reaction.

You just need to empathise and reflect. Here are some other phrases to reflect their emotions: **"Maybe you were a bit disappointed when you thought you needed a poo, but your body didn't push it out. Whatever happens with your wees and poos, we love you just as you are".**

"When a wee or a poo comes out and you didn't know it was going to, it sometimes makes you feel like you can't trust your body".

"I think you told me you hadn't wet yourself as you didn't want to get changed. You don't like the feeling of your wet clothes being peeled off you and then we have to wash you too which you don't like".

WORKING IN PARTNERSHIP WITH YOUR CHILDCARE PROVIDER

It's very important for children, and for you, to get the partnership right, not just between you and your child but with you and anyone else who is caring for your child. Ask your nursery or childminder what their approach is. More likely than not, they've had a lot of experience with this and hopefully they have a very positive approach. Get everyone on board with the approach of understanding the brain-body connection. Now this might be something that's quite new to a nursery, but it's still worth telling them that that's what you've been saying to your child. Tell them that you've been helping them to understand what body signals they're getting, in order to know when they need the toilet. Explain to them about descriptive praise and validating the child's feelings, particularly in respect to potty training.

Having a potty training buddy at nursery can help. Quite often children are potty training at similar times, not necessarily similar ages. You might suggest that they become buddies with another child to support each other. That can work really well. If your child is a little bit further along the line, they could be given the role of helping someone who's starting to train. Giving a child responsibility can really help them with their development as well.

Get your child really comfortable with the toilet area at their nursery. It's possible that there's a separate toilet area for those who have nappy changes and those who use the toilet. Your child may not have even been in that toilet area. Go in when you drop them off or when you collect them in the evening. Take a look around and ask them which toilet they like the best. If they're going to use a potty, ask them which potty they like the best. Do some hand-washing together, practice pulling off the toilet paper and flushing the loo.

Remember to send them with plenty of changes of clothes, even if they're not having many accidents at home, the change in environment can cause them to have accidents more frequently. Also remember nice, easy clothes to get on and off; elasticated waists, nothing tight, no buttons and clothes that you don't really worry about. Definitely take plenty of underwear.

Finally, hydrating properly at nursery (and home) is vital. Children often get very hot running around so you could remind your childcare provider that you want them to keep drinking throughout the session. Children need plenty of fluids.

Case Study

David got in touch with me because although his son Max was doing really well with potty training at home, at the end of the day at nursery, he was regularly presented with 4 bags of wet clothes. When I suggested he investigate more what the toilet procedure was at school, he discovered that Max found it really stressful to use the toilet at the same time as all the other children. He felt rushed and it was noisy. In consultation with the school, they arranged that Max could use the toilet before or after the standard class visit when it was just him or one other child. He had a preference for a certain cubicle and he was able to take his time in there. It was such a relief to David to pick Max up with no bags of wet clothes to take home.

SECTION 3: READY TO GO

You've reached Section Three: Ready to Go. I just want to run through the pre check list before you launch into potty training or maybe you've already started and you're taking a few steps back, in which case, still have a look at this list.

FINAL CHECKS

Is your child physically and emotionally ready? Now I know this is not always straightforward to know. We can start to doubt ourselves as parents, but I would really say trust your instinct. Trust yourself. If you think your child is ready, then I would say that you're probably right. I won't guarantee it, but there's a high chance that you're right. And if you have misjudged it, it's not a huge thing. You can course-correct. Take a few steps back into the process. That might mean that you wait a bit. Even if you feel like you need to potty train now, if your child isn't ready then put the brakes on it. You can wait a few days, weeks or months and come back to it.

If you've started introducing the potty and you feel that your child is just not engaged in it at all, try some of these things:

- Use the body diagram and talk about the mind body connection
- Play some fun music
- Get your child to pick out fun things for their busy bag
- Try getting a doll or a teddy and put them on the potty
- Read kid's potty training books with them
- Do role-play fully dressed and get them to tell you what to do

But if you really feel that they're just not ready, then, as I said above, come back to it another time. This isn't a source of shame or failure. It just wasn't quite the right timing.

Let's Just Assess that You Have Done Your Groundwork

Do you have a clear enough diary? Don't attempt it over a weekend where you've got 3 social engagements and a lot of work to catch up on. If you have done really effective preparation work, some children completely naturally transition into removing nappies and are dry and clean really fast, you may not even need to spend time at home with them. Others take longer. Even if you want your child dry for school, just be prepared, relaxed, and know that when they're ready, they will get it. Remember that you want this for your child, not in order to please somebody else or the school. Many children start nursery school not potty trained,just know that the important thing is getting it right for your child.

Do you have potties, pads and towels already? If you have a big house, you might want to have two or three potties dotted around. You might also want to put down some pads or blankets on seating.

REMEMBER

Don't Tell Your Child That Nappies are Babyish

You want them to see this as a positive step, a step towards independence, not that they have to move away from something that perhaps they should see as bad or shameful. So don't tell them that anyone wearing nappies is babyish. Tell them that this is such an exciting big stage for them.

Don't Swap Between Pull-ups and Underwear

Once you've started don't swap between pull-ups and underwear (*see FAQ section about trainer pants*). You will not be approaching night time dryness or naptime dryness yet so they will need a pull up or nappy for night and naps – unless you see that they are consistently dry after naps for about a week, in which case you can get rid of them too. Same for night time.

The key is that you are calm, understanding and trust your instinct as a parent. Many parents report that around day 3 they are ready to give up but they so often get their child over the hump, it all clicks into place and they never look back, so don't give up too soon!

Don't compare them to another child who is potty trained. Just focus on the progress your child is making. You also have to be careful with your tone of voice. So don't say, "Edward doesn't wear nappies so you should be like him", or "Olivia doesn't have accidents, she always uses the potty". I know that the intention is to motivate your child to want to be like their friends but what comes across is that your child isn't as good as their friend. Once you start to make progress you can say things like, "It is so great that you are making wees and poos on the potty like Edward", that is different.

SHOULD YOU USE REWARDS?

Some other books and parents say that rewards work well – i.e. rewarding with a chocolate or a sticker every time they use the potty. I find that a child will often try to squeeze out teeny drop in order to get the reward and or they feel like they've failed because they haven't produced anything, so they didn't get the reward. You really want them to be doing it for them, not just in order to get the treat. So I don't advise this method.

The collaborative, positive approach combined with engaging your child with the science is much more powerful. I can see the logic for some parents, the reinforcement of the positive with the reward but parents following my method say that their children want to use the potty because they need to go, they feel physical relief when they go and they are proud of themselves. You can be really enthusiastic with your praise and use that as a reward, **"You should feel so proud of yourself. Your body told you to hold it till you reached the potty and then let it out and look what a wonderful poo you produced".** This will have a much longer-lasting effect than the sticker or sweet.

THE IMPORTANCE OF STAYING CALM

Now what most parents do is start off nice and calm, but if the process takes longer than they're expecting, they start to get frustrated and run out of patience. They often don't realise that they're getting cross. You might show it in your tone of voice or the physical way you move a child. Children need to feel that they are okay with who they are and that they're not trying to perform in order to gain your love. If you feel frustrated, then ask someone else to take over or walk away to breathe for a few minutes. Taking a break for yourself can make a big difference.

Ask yourself, "What do I need to do to stay calm?". Potty training takes time and there will be accidents. Children lose focus, they're absorbed in other things and they have accidents. We have to remind ourselves that learning to use the potty is a complicated skill and they are learning. You will stay calmer if you manage your own expectations - expect accidents, expect it to take a while for them to get it and expect days when you have regression.

POSITIVE THINGS TO DO

Positive Language

Do use descriptive praise and reflective listening to validate your child's feelings. Use a light, kind, easy tone. Getting as fluent as you can with those two key skills will really help you. Go back to the **Get Set** section to remind yourself of the language to use.

Positive Body Talk

Remember to keep referring to their brain / body connection. Show the body diagram. (You can download this diagram from the My Parenting Solutions - **www.myparentingsolutions.com/pottyresources.**) Point to the body parts and describe your own process of elimination.

When you talk about wee and poo, you want to make the separation between the brain and body. Say things like:

"Is your bladder telling your brain that it needs a wee?". Also when they sit on a potty you say, **"Does your brain need to tell your bladder to relax to let the wee out?".**

"The muscles in your tummy (or bowel/colon) give signals to your brain and when the poo needs to come out, the muscles push the poo out. You can talk to your muscles to tell them to push the poo out when you sit on the potty".

"You can also tell the muscles in your bladder or in your bottom to hold on until you reach the potty, so you make it in time".

Positive Play

Use play to help encourage your child. As a parent, be mindful of what type of play your child really enjoys the most. So, for example, **Small-world play:** you could use figures to do pretend play with a bathroom situation.

Construction: they could build a bathroom area with bricks or Lego.

Role-play: engage role-play using one of their toys, a doll or a teddy and tell them they might be going to try the potty. You can buy little toy potties that some children really like, so dolly or teddy goes too. You might also ask your child how teddy or dolly is feeling - this will give you some really useful information as children are often much more able to describe what they are feeling via a third party object like a toy (or via a story).

Music and movement: you might pick out special potty music (at the end of the book is a list of potty-specific songs that kids like, but you don't have to stick to those, you can pick your own too. Some children respond well to doing a special potty dance, this could be before they use the potty or afterwards to celebrate.

Generally have some fun with it. Use funny voices or play acting. You can engage their favourite character to get involved, either in role-play using their imagination or if they have a physical toy they love, the toy can come to the potty with them.

Investigations: Children love science and getting them involved in a demonstration can really bring things to life for them and makes it more interesting. I recommend doing the **Balloon Experiment** below.

"Our son responded so well to Camilla's balloon experiment. He went from 6 accidents a day to barely any in a really short space of time."

Justina O'Donnell

THE BALLOON EXPERIMENT

The purpose of this experiment is to show a child how their body stores water and what happens when the water is released as wee. Some (not all) children are fascinated by this and it really helps them understand the physical process so much better.

A child over the age of two can hold approximately 180ml or 6oz of water. Show them how much their bladder holds by doing the balloon experiment.

You will need:

- A measuring jug
- 180ml water
- A funnel
- A balloon
- Yellow food dye (if you have some).

1.

2.

3.

4.

Instructions:

Fill a jug together with 180ml of water (you could add a couple of drops of yellow food dye to the water to make it look more authentic). Then get a funnel and a balloon and fill the balloon with the water in the jug. That shows them what their bladder capacity is.

Talk about the different times of day when they're going to need to use the potty. Talk to them about the fact that when they first start, they're probably going to need to go more frequently than you do because their bladder capacity is growing and it doesn't hold as much as a grown up.

Show them the diagram and point to their body at the same time. **"Here is your mouth, water goes in and it goes down through your body. Your body uses the liquid – like a plant needs water – then the rest goes into your bladder and your body needs to let it out", "When I go to the toilet, my bladder feels full and it sends me a message that I need to release the muscles that let out the wee".** You can talk to your child with the aid of the anatomical diagram. Children find these kinds of things interesting to know.

STOP AND GO SIGNS

Not all children will respond to this, but you can test it out. The way you use them is if you've got a child that gets very absorbed in what they're doing, you might explain to them that you're going to use these two signs. One is to show them when you want them to stop what they're doing, and the other is to remind them they might need to go toilet.

Remember that if your child is saying they don't need to go, you just need to accept it, even if they have an accident soon after. If you force it, they will resist you and you don't want to have battles over anything. You could try having a drinking competition to get them to drink some more or give them a nice water bottle so you can measure how much they've had, particularly in the early stages that will help give them the urge to go.

You can download these signs from My Parenting Solutions: www.myparentingsolutions.com/pottyresources.

THE FIRST DAYS WITHOUT A NAPPY

Some children, especially those properly prepared, are very easy to potty train and will pick up the skill without any problems at all, others find it much harder to master. It is difficult to predict how they will respond but what we do know is that the greater your trust in them and the more relaxed and confident you are about it, the better they will respond. Followimg are my recommendations based on research and on the experience of the hundreds of clients I've helped.

Let them run around naked for the first few days without wearing any underwear. Why do we do this? Because they need to be able to feel the sensation and if they are wearing pants, it can feel like a nappy to them, therefore they are more likely to forget to notice their signals and have accidents. Remember to talk about the body parts and the connection between their brain and the body and look at the anatomical diagram.

Talk about all these parts and point to them on their body. Get them to point them out to you. Let your child have some choices throughout the day to give them that feeling of power, let them choose - the books that you read, the games that they play, what colour cup they want to drink from, things like that. Perhaps they could even choose what they have for mealtimes on these first few days (within limits). As I've said already, some children get weeing and pooing on the potty really quickly and others take much longer, each child is so different. Restrict screen time in the early stages because when they're watching a screen, they're less likely to want to stop what they're doing and secondly, they are so absorbed that they will often fail to notice their body signal.

Your job is to watch them like a hawk for signals they are giving that they need a wee or poo. You then talk about what you see rather than constantly asking, "Do you need a wee?" which will annoy them. So instead you can reflect on what you see and give an instruction, **"You are hopping up and down, come with me and we can march to the potty like a soldier".**

Routine

It can be helpful to map out the different times of the day for regular visits to the potty or toilet. This can be:

- When they first wake up in the morning
- Before they go out of the house
- Before or after each meal
- Before bath time and before bedtime

If you get them into a routine with this it is very helpful. They don't need to have produced anything, but the requirement is that they try. Children who respond well to routines will thrive on this. You can make a visual time table to show them when they need to try.

Case Study

Jason and Nicola decided to potty train Louis (aged 2½) during a summer holiday. This can work well as long as the holiday is in one place and you have time to focus on your child. They set up for success by bringing along a potty that fitted Louis well. They had already done naked time at home before the bath, and they'd read potty training books and packed a 'busy bag' to take with them. In the first few days there were many more wees and poos off the potty than on it, which Jason found very hard to deal with. He told Nicola that they must have got the timing wrong as Louis was having so many accidents. They decided to stick with it as Louis was happy about the whole thing and they'd managed to catch a few wees and one poo on the potty. After a few days, things started to click for Louis. Having let him have the sensation of doing a naked wee, he started noticing a dribble or the feeling of a poo waiting to come out and he'd call one of his parents. They said the key was not to rush at him and grab him to get to the potty on time. They said things like, "That's great. Your body signals are getting so much stronger. Let's get you on the potty to let out your wee or poo". They discovered that if they shouted, "Wait", or "Hold on", it was frightening for Louis, so they needed to be very calm about it.

The night before, you're going to start potty training without a nappy, ask your child what's going to happen tomorrow.

"Do you remember what is going to happen tomorrow?", "That's right, you are going to be so grown up and not wear a nappy". "You can run around naked and learn how to do your wees and poos in a potty". You might also use some of your reflective listening skills and say, **"That might feel a bit strange for you. You've worn a nappy for a long time, and it will feel different. I think you're actually going to find it's fun."**

Ideally spend at least the first 3-4 days at home, based in one or two rooms. You need to be making it as easy as possible for your child. If you do need to go out, try to stay very close to home for the following 3-4 days as well. It's so hard to predict, but you will probably need a little longer before you can go on long car or train journeys without accidents.

The first morning when you remove their nappy, try sitting your child on the potty or the toilet. Play a song, or run water from the tap and wait for a few minutes. See if something comes out. If nothing is produced, carry on the morning routine with no underwear. It really is better if they can be naked - you can explain that their special underwear is for when they have learnt to use the potty.

Have breakfast with plenty of fluids. Have a drinking race, let them play and avoid screens. You want to avoid your own screens too as you want to observe your child like a hawk for signs they might need to go.

Here are some warning signs to look out for:

- A far-away look
- They stop talking and go quiet
- They move from one foot to another

- They let out little farts
- They move their hips around
- They wiggle their toes
- They put their hand to their bottom
- They touch their genital area
- Their breathing can speed up or slow down
- They look from side to side, moving their head

Hopefully you'll have identified some of these signs already. If you see them and you've got a hunch it is a potty signal, say to your child, **"Come with me, it looks like you need the potty".**

This is where your creativity needs to come into play. You can sing, you can hop on one leg, use a funny voice, get their favourite toy and speak through the toy as if the toy is communicating with your child. Move the potty to them or keep it close by so that they don't have to go far.

Dealing with FOMO - a very common reason that your child will refuse to come to the potty is that they have FOMO - fear of missing out. They won't express it this way but they'll resist stopping what they are doing. What you can say is, **"The game is going to stay here and you can come straight back to it"** or, **"You can still do your colouring when you come back"**. Remember that screens absorb their full attention so either have no screens in the early stages or expect accidents when they are watching.

Creating a Routine

After between 45 - 60 minutes, try using the stop and go signs and ask them to go and have a try. Keep this up every 45 - 60 minutes. We don't want this to become a nag, but nevertheless, in the early stages, you'll need to be very observant of their signals and help them to use the potty or toilet. You'll be prompting more in the first few days without the nappy. Prompting isn't asking them, "Do you need to potty?" as they are most likely going to say "No". It is observing and making a requirement:

"Oh, it's time for snack, so we have to use the potty first - do you remember our rule?", or **"I see you moving from one foot to another, ok, it's potty time - I bet you can't get there first!".**

You can also say, **"Remember to tell mummy/daddy (or anyone else looking after them) when your body is giving you a sign".**

Get them to check in with their signals and say things like, **"Tell mummy when your bladder feels full", "Tell daddy when you feel a poo in your bottom".**

Your own use of a phone or an iPad or a computer should be kept to a minimum too. This is time to devote to your child, to have time with them and to make it a nice, enjoyable process that you both have good feelings about. Periodically ask them every 45 - 60 minutes if their body is giving them a signal but don't force it.

Watch for their nonverbal signs and when you see them you might tell them that their body is telling you something, **"I think your body is giving you a sign, let's go and see what happens on the potty. Try to use your muscles to hold your wee in until you reach the potty".**

Do this with a really calm voice, you don't want to scare them. When they produce something, celebrate. Say, "You should be proud of yourself", rather than, "I'm proud of you". You want them to feel intrinsic and internal motivation and pride, rather than it being something to please you. If the opposite happens, if they don't produce something, they can tend to feel like they've disappointed you, which is not what you want at all. You can say something like, **"It takes a long time to learn this. Sometimes nothing comes out and that's fine"**. If they don't get to the potty on time and have an accident, just say, **"Oh, that's normal. You're learning about your body. The wee/poo came out sooner than you thought it would".**

GIRLS VS BOYS

People might tell you there's a big difference between potty training boys and girls, but I'm not convinced. Sometimes different things can motivate them. Boys may like to wee outside so you can make a game of doing a wee up a tree. Girls can wee outside too - you just might need to get involved and hold them in a squatting position. Boys tend to be a little more impulsive and high energy so might be more inclined to run off rather than using the potty. Girls may like to take social cues from others so might be motivated to copy friends who are potty trained. But if you use the positive approach I'm suggesting in this whole book, it doesn't matter what sex they are, they'll be motivated to get going successfully.

Normalising the Experience

We want to make this a natural and normal process and not something that has any form of shame or embarrassment around it. Children might not like seeing their 'special poo' come out but if you are positive about it, they will take the lead from you. We can make a bit of a face about poo, or fuss about the smell, but children need to feel that that producing a poo is something they should be proud of. This will help avoid any potential issues they may have around withholding poos or wees in or becoming constipated from not wanting to let it out - see the section on **Withholding** in **Section 4** if this is a problem for you.

So, if they do a poo on the floor or in their underwear, don't make a fuss. Take a look at the poo, say something admiringly like, **"Wow, look what your body made. That is all the bits you don't need and the rest of the food makes you grow big and strong"**. Get them to help flush it and say goodbye to 'Mr Poo'. And you might say something like, **"Next time, do you think it would like to meet the potty?".**

It can feel shocking to them when wee pours down their legs, but if we respond with enthusiasm, they will feel good about it. **"Hey, look at that, your wee is coming out. Your bladder relaxed and let it out. Next time you might be able to get it into the potty, what do you think?".**

DEALING WITH ACCIDENTS

When your child has an accident, make no fuss and don't say anything critical afterwards. You could say, **"You are still learning to notice your signals. I think you were so busy with your game that you forgot to notice".** Remind them that it takes a while to learn how their body works and what their body's signals are.

I know it is easy to start positive and if potty training has gone on longer than you'd expected, you can start to get impatient. I really get it. I wish I'd known about this method of potty training with my second child Felix. He was one of those who used to hide to poo. When he came out from behind the sofa with his pants swaying and a smell emanating from his rear-end I'd sigh, hold my nose and say, "OH FELIX, why didn't you tell me, now we've got to change you". We spent so many months getting more and more frustrated with him and making no progress. It was when I discovered you can teach a child how their body works and the brain-body connection that it all clicked for him.

We want to give our children the message over and over again that mistakes are fine and we learn from them. If they feel any shame about having an accident they will begin to deny they've had one, hide their underwear, get upset or aggressive about it or pretend they don't care, when they do. If you have experienced any of these responses with your child, know that you can get back on the right track with them. If they have negative feelings around making mistakes, this can prevent them from trying things or from taking risks in the future.

Cleaning Up From Accidents

Let your child be involved in the clean-up. They can help to wipe the floor and put the wet clothes in a bag or the laundry basket and all the time, you'll be praising each small step.

"You managed to take off wet clothes, that's not easy is it? And you knew to put them into the laundry basket. You found your clean clothes and now you are putting them back on! So independent!".

You can get them to put on clean clothes independently or give them some help to do it. This isn't as a punishment, it's just collaborative.

They're taking some responsibility and they are getting involved in the process, that's helpful for them. Before or after they've cleaned up, have them sit back again on the potty as they may have a little more to do. With every step, remember to use **Descriptive Praise** as described in **Section 2.**

During the first few days or weeks without a nappy, expect accidents. Don't be discouraged by them. Don't give up when your child wees on the floor or on the carpet, the carpets can always be cleaned. If it is really bothering you, you might want to put some protective covering down. Make it a priority to help your child master the skill and remind yourself that carpets can be washed with some soapy water or professionally cleaned.

Can I Leave the House in the First Few Days?

Observe your child's response carefully. If progress seems slow, reassure yourself that this stage takes time. For some kids, going outside isn't a problem and they can make the transition easily, for others it can really throw them. I don't like to prescribe hard and fast rules, but I would say If you do go out, don't go making a long car journey or a trip to a museum. Keep things local and take a potty with you. Tell your child they can take the potty somewhere private if that helps.

Should I Use a Pull-up?

I don't recommend using pull-ups when you go out. They give the child a confusing message, "I trust you to know when to use the potty at home but I don't trust you outside the house". Pull-ups are so absorbent that kids just don't recognise when they've wet themselves. Use protective pads for the car seat and the buggy and take a change of clothes or two. If your child has an accident when you are out - it really isn't a big deal.

The more confident we are in their abilities, the better results you're going to get. Take plenty of spare clothing and wipes and as time goes on, the accidents will reduce, and their control and understanding will greatly increase. You will feel so good about this and so will they.

A few more points on the first days of removing the nappy, keep your child naked for as much time as you can and keep using all the techniques to help you reach your goal. The more patient you are, the better. And I really recommend using any form of relaxation techniques for yourself because that can help you just chill out and be more of a relaxed parent. This is a collaborative approach. As well as being led by your child, you are also leading them. So for example, you can have some requirements such as everybody has to visit the toilet before leaving home, or everyone goes to the toilet before or after a meal.

How Much Should You Prompt?

Should I prompt or should I let my child take the lead? You are working towards your child noticing their body signals and asking you to take them to the potty, ultimately they will take themselves. At first however you will need to give some gentle reminders. Say, **"Remember to tell me when you feel the wee or poo coming"**, you will want to check in quite frequently – about every 45 minutes in the beginning and that can extend once they have got the hang of it. When you check in you'll say something like, **"Does the wee need to come out? What is your body telling you?"**. If you see them jiggling or holding onto their crotch you can say, **"I think your body is giving you a signal, come and sit on the potty to see if the wee or poo is ready to come out".**

HOW TO GET POO IN THE POTTY!

I wanted to do a separate section on poo, just to make things clear and give you some extra ideas and support with it. Firstly, is your child regular? If your child has a regular poo time, then put in your routine that they sit on the potty at the time when they usually go. Not all children are predictable, but very often it's when they first wake up, 20 minutes after a meal or after the bath when their muscles are relaxed. Set a timer on your phone to remind you to give them poo time. Get them engaged and give them time to sit.

Where possible sit with them reading a book or listening to some songs. They could have their busy bag which contains things that they like that occupy them. It could also be useful to give them a stress ball or squeeze or a balloon to blow into. This relaxes the muscles in their bottom. Not all children are predictable and catching a poo on the potty can take a while and be frustrating. Cleaning wee is quite simple and poo is messier especially if they have sat it in it.

For the best sitting position their knees should be higher than their waist. That's why a potty is good for poos because it gets them into the right position. Talk about letting the muscles push out the poo. Their body is doing the work. It's not unusual for a child to ask for their nappy for poos for quite some time during potty training. Praise them because they have noticed that their body is telling them they need to poo. Don't battle about this, let them have a nappy to poo in if it seems important to them. It can cause so many problems if you fight about it. Working with them collaboratively, you will eventually help them to lose their fear of pooing on the potty or into the toilet.

"I was so resentful of stealth poos that I used to get really angry with my daughter. When I changed the approach and validated how much she liked privacy, she started to use the potty I left in her hiding spot."
Eleanor O'Brien

Stealth Poos

Some children will disappear behind a sofa or into another room to quietly do the poo in their pants (this was my son). If they have a regular spot, then make sure you leave a potty in the spot. Talk this over with your child. **"I know you like to go quietly to do a poo don't you? So I'm going to leave the potty in your favourite place"**, then ask the question **"Now you are potty training, where do you need the poo to go?".** Those introverts who like privacy might also like you to make them a 'poo tent', you can put a blanket over chairs and put the potty in the middle which gives them complete privacy. Worth a try if they are persistently hiding to poo and not using the potty.

DAY 3-7 WITHOUT A NAPPY

So onwards to approximately days three to seven 3-7, (and this is really approximate), I wanted to give you ideas about how to take things further. You can test out putting them in pants if you haven't done this till now. If they've been doing well and regress with pants on, then you might need to go back a stage and do as much naked time as possible or let them wear baggy clothes without pants (underwear) underneath.

When they go to nursery or childcare, take time to talk to their teacher and inform them of your child's progress. They will probably have what we call a key worker. Somebody that's responsible for your child. That person may not work every day that your child goes in, so make sure that the communication is good with everyone. Keep the nappies off and take plenty of changes of clothes. Tell the staff what's been working when at home and make sure that all staff are involved.

Go with your child on the first day, have them practise pulling their pants down and sitting. Make sure your child has a full water bottle so that they're properly hydrated. And if they still want a nappy for a poo, don't fight it. Tell the childcare provider about this and praise them for telling someone they need a poo.

If your child isn't at nursery but stays at home with you or a nanny, then start to venture out as soon as you feel you can. (This is usually after 3-5 days but totally varies from child to child).

Using a Potty or a Toilet Outside the House

Take a potty and a few changes of clothes with you wherever you go and let your child know that you have them with you. They may transition really well to using a toilet wherever they go, but just in case, have a potty with you and make sure that your child knows that you have it. Always tell your child that they can stop and go any time and you're going to be there to help them. Talk about how their muscles and bladder are getting stronger and stronger and able to hold on for longer and longer.

If you have a noise-sensitive child, when you take them out try to take them to a quiet place and give them warning about where you're going to go. Watch out for automatic flushes in public toilets as some children can be frightened of these. You can, if you want to, take a post it note and cover the automatic flush, this will prevent it from flushing before you're ready. You can invest in a portable potty called a 'Pottette' which some parents like. I personally never used one of those but parents do rate them highly.

WHAT TO EXPECT BEYOND THE FIRST FEW WEEKS

Expect accidents and don't go back to pull ups or nappies (other than for naptime and bedtime) unless it just isn't working well and your child is completely miserable. Remember to approach the accidents without any form of criticism and avoid a negative tone of voice, or sighs and frowning expressions, if they have accidents. I understand how difficult this is. If you feel upset or despondent, walk away and take a few breaths. Always take a change of clothes, take your travel potty and let your child know that you have it.

Case Study

Colette and Dan started potty training Jack just before their second baby was born. They wanted to get it over and done with before the baby and Jack was due to start nursery a few weeks later. Jack was extremely reluctant about the whole thing. He wasn't interested in any of the books they'd bought and he didn't want to accompany either of them to the toilet. They bought him a potty that played a tune and he screamed the place down when they tried to get him to sit on it. Colette and Dan got in touch in a bit of a state about the whole issue. I suggested that Jack was not only picking up on their anxiety about the time pressure regarding starting nursery, but that the arrival of the baby was going to be tough for Jack to deal with and they weren't going to be able to give him the time and attention he needed. Together we decided that they would press pause and come back to potty training at a later date. Their nursery school agreed it was too much pressure on Jack to have him trained before he started. Once baby Esme was 3 months old and Jack had had time to adjust to his new school and his baby sister, Colette and Dan went back to potty training but this time with a plan in place. They took it slowly, starting off with engaging Jack in games, looking at my anatomical diagram and discussing how his body worked. They did potty-practice with his clothes on and then moved to sitting naked on the potty before the bath. The whole process was relaxed and fun and within a few days Jack was asking to use the potty and would also be led by Colette and Dan when they could see he needed to go.

Helping Your Child to Train Their Body to 'Hold On'

Parents can get frustrated if a child has an accident before they reach the potty. What we so often forget to take into consideration is that the term 'hold onto it' might not mean anything to a child. So reiterate often, **"Our muscles can hold wee and poo in until you reach the potty. Then we can let it out in the right place".** Some children take to the process really fast, especially if you've done the groundwork and others take longer. Stay patient and keep working on the positive language to build your connection with your child.

Night-time Training

In my opinion, night time dryness is driven by the maturity of their bladder and its capacity. This grows with age and varies from child to child. Some books will tell you to remove nappies for day, night and naptime all at once. I personally feel that is too much pressure on the child and the daily washing and drying of bedlinen can push parents over the edge. I advise that you don't expect night-time dryness until AT LEAST 6 months after they are reliably dry during the day. Some kids are such deep sleepers that they sleep through the signals, others have a small bladder capacity. You can try cutting back on fluids before bedtime or getting them to do a 'dream-wee' when you go to bed, but generally I advise waiting till it happens naturally.

You may find that at this point your child is making fantastic day (and even night-time) progress. They recognise their body signals, will take your lead when you suggest they need the potty and you are confident that things are all headed in the right direction. The next chapter covers troubleshooting for when things don't go quite according to plan.

SECTION 4: TROUBLESHOOTING AND FAQS

If it occurs, there's always some sort of psychological link with regression and in this chapter, there are ideas for you to help solve issues you have. There are also frequently asked questions from other parents. The final part is a section on withholding. Some children may withhold their poos or wees and there are solutions for that problem in this chapter.

Remember it's a shared journey, not one entirely led by you. And nor is it entirely led by them. So, if you go back to the section on reflective listening and validating their feelings, I would pretty much assure you that somewhere within that are examples that you could use to help.

If you have a child who is getting distressed and upset about potty training at any stage, you may think it is better to pause potty training for a while, this will take the pressure off everyone for a bit. Remember it's not a failure if you need to do this. Use validation to reflect their feelings at this stage, then you might say, "I think you'd be happier if we stopped potty training for a while and we can come back to it a little later".

Next are questions frequently asked and common causes of regression.

FREQUENTLY ASKED QUESTIONS

1. Is it Better to Potty Train in the Summer?

The summer can be great because it's warmer and you are able to let your children be naked outside. However, if you feel that your child is showing signs of readiness in the winter, then there is no point delaying till the summer. Ideally you can let them run around without anything much on for the first few days so just keep the house warm and let them do that in the winter-time.

2. Are Girls Easier Than Boys?

Not in my experience. It's really to do with how you motivate your child. And it is also to do with their temperament and their character.

3. Is There a Perfect Time to Start Training?

There's never a perfect time for anything, but I would just say trust your intuition, put some energy and time into it. Hopefully you'll get the timing right, but there's never a perfect time. There's never a time where you have no distractions, nothing's going on and your child is absolutely looking like they're completely 100% ready. But the preparation that you put in will get the results.

4. Should My Child's Nursery Take the Lead?

No, nurseries will tell you that it is up to the parent or whoever is spending the most 1:1 time with the child to decide. They will want to work with you. They might say that they've seen signs of readiness and suggest you get started but they want parents to initiate the process. If somebody in the main caring role at home suggests that the child is showing signs of readiness, then let them take the lead.

5. What if We're About to Go on Holiday?

Holidays can be a really great place to potty train your child. There's less going on. If you're in a place with some privacy, say you're renting a holiday home or you're in a hotel where you're going to get to spend lots of time with your child, it can be a great time to do it because everybody's feeling relaxed. If it's a warm holiday, there's that chance to run around naked. I successfully trained my first child on holiday. So yes, I would say holidays can be good, but don't plan the holiday around it in case you can't get the timing quite right.

6. Should I Use Trainer Pants?

Trainer pants act like a pull-up, so a child isn't getting the same sensation that they get with ordinary underwear. They are also quite expensive and I don't think they are necessary.

7. My Child is Over Three. Have I Missed the Window?

You definitely haven't. You go through the sections in the same way. These steps work just as well with a child over three. You may find a little bit more resistance with a child over three because they've had longer in nappies, but you can definitely get there and sometimes, because they're that bit older and they have greater bladder capacity, they train really quickly. Have no shame around it. Some parents have that awful feeling like, "My child is so old and everybody else's child is trained". Maybe you've started and failed and you're really feeling guilty about the whole process. Put all that aside and just focus on what will work to motivate your child, get them involved, collaborate with them, even problem-solve with them because they are going to have more cognitive ability.

"Amy completely refused the toilet anywhere but home which meant we couldn't go far. We discovered she was brave enough to use a friend's toilet so we started with that and progressed bit by bit . What a relief to sort it out!"

Lucas, dad of Amy

8. My Child is Frightened of Using the Potty or Toilet

Some children are happy with a potty, but they're really frightened of using a toilet. Others are frightened of both. Go gently on this one. Give them the opportunity to sit on the potty or toilet, with their clothes on as many times as they like. Try to break down what the fear is about by making some guesses, **"I wonder if you are worried you are going to fall in?"** or, **"Maybe when you sat on the potty and it tipped over, you got a fright?"** or, **"Perhaps you are scared of seeing your poo or wee in drop into the toilet?"** (that's a common one). Don't make it into more of an issue that it needs to be, show your child that you are confident they won't always be scared. So although you aren't going to say, "Don't be scared," as that denies their emotions, you can say, **"I know you will soon feel brave enough to try again".** This won't last forever and if you want to get help, reach out to me via my website **www.myparentingsolutons.com.**

9. My Child Refuses to Go to the Toilet When They're Out

Clarify what it is they're refusing to do and what they're resisting. It might be they've been frightened by a flush, or the smell or it could be just the unfamiliar environment. So it's a question of slowly getting them used to it and maybe thinking creatively. You could take a nice room spray to make the toilet smell more familiar. It could be that they've had a frightening experience at one time and you didn't realise. See if you can find out with some gentle probing. Don't ask directly but be curious, **"I wonder if you got a fright when you used another toilet?"**. Validate the fact that home feels safer, **"You prefer to use the toilet at home because it's cosier. You don't like using other toilets"**. Then you might mention the problem, **"The problem is that you get so upset when you need to go but you won't try anywhere else. What could we do about that?"**. Engaging kids in solution-finding empowers them to come up with ideas.

HERE ARE SOME COMMON ISSUES THAT I TOUCHED ON IN THE BOOK:

A Child Who Will Only Poo in a Nappy

Now, I've mentioned this at other points during the book, it's a very common one. It is to do with security and it is to do with fear of letting go of the poo - it might be linked with a bad experience of pooing in the potty, or it might be triggered by experiencing constipation. You want to avoid a child holding their poos as that can turn into a nasty cycle of withholding and pain, leading into constipation (this is covered a bit further on in this chapter).

Start off encouraging them to sit on the potty to do the poo in their nappy. From there you can open the tabs so that the nappy becomes looser on them. You can progress to cutting a hole in the nappy, so the poo comes through the hole. All the time explaining what you're doing to the child, getting their collaboration with it, being gentle and showing that you've understood that it's the reason they will only want to do a poo in the nappy is that they feel fearful.

Talk about poos in a really positive way, showing them that getting rid of the poo is getting rid of a waste product because all the good part has gone into their body to give them energy and help them grow.

Some of the songs, books and apps can help here. You can find these resources on **www.myparentingsolutions.com/pottyresources** in a booklet.

Refuses to go to the toilet and then has an accident shortly afterwards.

You want a child to be motivated towards doing something. So it's about not shaming them. You're going to say things like, **"Oh dear. I think you were so busy doing whatever it was that you were doing that you forgot to notice you needed to go. I could see it because I saw you jiggling around and that's what the potty dance showed me. I think you refused to come because you were enjoying your game too much".** And then you might say, **"What do you think you need to do next time?".**

Hard as it is, if this goes on for longer than you expected, you always need to use that positive tone of voice. I know this is difficult because what tends to happen with parents is that you start off positive and then when this happens repeatedly, you start to lose your patience. But when you get into an impatient cycle, it's only going to demotivate your child. Remember that you will get there and the more confidence you have in your child about this, the more they're going to be able to get it. Don't reprimand them because it only makes them resentful and less willing to listen to you. Keep observing their body signals and commenting on what you see instead of repeatedly asking them if they need the toilet. Praise all the small steps of progress, **"You nearly reached the potty today", "You did three wees in the potty today, that's two more than yesterday".**

REGRESSION

You might have started potty training, found it really easy and then your child reverts back to having a lot of accidents. This is regression and you need to figure out what the causes of that regression might be. Some of the causes might be a change in circumstances. Have you moved house?

Or, are you going to move house? Children, and particularly sensitive children, will often have a physical reaction to this change. This physical reaction might be more frequent poos or wee accidents. It's a delicate area, but it needs to be said that relationship conflict can cause regression, particularly if children are being exposed to it more than normal.

Remember that children are like sponges. Sponges for the positive, and also sponges for the negative. They absorb and take everything in and often something seemingly small can trigger a regression. Everything from a new teacher, parent going back to work or travelling, starting a new school, a friend leaving the class or a new person joining the class, a change in childcare, a new bedroom – any of these types of things can trigger a regression. It doesn't mean to say that it'll always be this way. Use what I taught you in the chapter on validating emotions. Take some guesses and put things into words for them, **"I wonder if you are missing Jacinta, your old teacher, and it feels strange that Jackie takes you to the toilet".**

"It's hard starting a new school (or moving into a new class). It can make you feel nervous and forget to ask to go to the toilet".

"When mummy has to travel for work and daddy looks after you, I think you feel anxious and that makes you forget to notice you need the potty".

Regression and New Baby

You may have had a new baby and your child had chugged along and been perfectly well potty trained and then suddenly that baby becomes more engaging and your child realises that the baby is a bit more of a threat. They are aware that other people are engaging with the baby much more and that can be a trigger for the regression. The way to deal with that is to tell your child that you understand that it's hard having a new baby in the family. Explain to your child that he or she may have feelings of jealousy or resentment towards the baby. By saying this you help them to deal with the emotion and be more resilient about coping with the baby. You won't reduce the emotion by telling your child that they shouldn't feel that way.

Travelling

When children travel, they often regress with their potty training because there's so much else going on. It can help to involve your child and get them to help you prepare for the trip. But if they still regress, know that it is probably temporary.

The Absence of a Parent

Maybe one parent has had to go away for extended periods of time for work or maybe they're spending time in hospital. That's going to have an emotional impact on your child. The more you talk about it, the more you help them adapt to it and they'll feel like their emotions have been understood.

Someone in Their World Hasn't Been Treating Your Child in the Right Way

If you've got an unexpected regression that you really can't figure out, look out for other causes for it. You might want to look at if somebody involved in their childcare, an older sibling or an older child that they have contact with, hasn't been treating them kindly. These things can go on without us being aware.

The Illness or Death of a Loved One

This can include family, friends and even pets. This can also cause regression. In these instances, we need to help the child process their emotions and just deal sensitively with accidents.

Case Study

Sari and Kasem got in touch because they were puzzled by their daughter Tara's regression. They potty trained Tara during the summer holiday with relative ease and when she went back to nursery in September she developed a terrible fear of using the potty so they decided to put her back in nappies. Sari learnt how to validate and uncover Tara's feelings and one day Tara said, "Lisa shout at me when I do wee". It turned out that her key worker (who had left by then) had treated Tara roughly and humiliated her for having an accident. That had been the cause of the regression. It took a long time and a lot of patience to un-do the harm, but Sari and Kasem got there in the end.

WITHHOLDING WEES

Some children wear underwear but will still only wee once they have a nappy on. Some children will hold onto it until bedtime! This means that they have such strong control over the muscles, the ones that release the waste from the bladder, or these muscles are working too hard and won't relax. What will usually be causing this is a fear of letting go into the potty or the toilet. And if that is the case, I would start off with a lot of discussion about how their body works and show them the diagrams. Describe the process of letting wee out as a really good thing. It's a waste product. You could even do something like demonstrate with a plant. If you take a potted plant, put loads of water through it, they'll see that some will be released into the bottom, into the little tray that you've put underneath. Sometimes that can help them understand what the wee is for.

If the fear still remains, I would suggest that you put an open nappy over the potty every time they wee. In some cases, you may need to put them in a nappy and then have the requirement that they sit on the potty to wee. But it is important that you help them let go of the fear.

You can also put some lavender drops in the toilet, if they're able to use the toilet, or put some drops in a little bit of water in the potty and that can help the muscles relax. You could also put lavender drops in a glass or one of those infusers near where the potty is. The smell of the lavender can sometimes help the muscles relax, you can also put a tap on when they wee, as the sound of water can sometimes stimulate the muscles to relax. Encourage extra intake of fluids. It's so important that they have lots of fluids to help this process along.

Another option is to let them have a wee in the bath and talk about how the warm water relaxes their muscles. The more relaxed you are about it, the better. Stay positive and calm and it will get better.

WITHHOLDING POOS

If a child has a painful poo, it can start a cycle of withholding because the child doesn't want to feel the pain from doing a poo. Doing a poo will have at some point been frightening or painful in order for this cycle to have started. Withholding means that their muscles want to push the poo out, but they hold it in with the sphincter muscles because they're afraid of the pain.

Sometimes withholding can even have started when they were still a baby. Think back to the early stages when it might have first started. Quite often it's because they'd been ill, they became dehydrated and they found it really hard to push that poo out. Tell your child the story of what happened. Use all your reflective listening skills to acknowledge how difficult it is for your child. **"I know that you're fearful of poo coming out. I know that you've had an experience of it being painful and I know that that's hard for you".**

Using mud play can give them a sensory experience of hard poo and soft poo. Find some mud, show them what hard mud looks like. Add water to it and let them squish it so that they see how much softer it is when water is added to it. Get them to squeeze it in their hands so they can see that if this was poo it wouldn't hurt. You can also do this with dry clay.

Children need to be sitting comfortably to poo, ideally in a squatting position with knees above their waist level. That position is best done on a potty, as toilet seats make it hard to get in a good position for a child who suffers with constipation or withholding. Try regular sitting after meals on the potty as part of your daily routine. Keep track of any time they have done a poo and mark it on a chart. If any sort of pattern emerges, then you want to get them to have their sit times just before they might be about to do a poo. Make sure that they've got plenty of things to occupy them or you can sit with them and read them a story. Ten minutes is a minimum length of time to give the body enough time to relax. Another solution is to get them to blow bubbles or blow up a balloon while sitting on the potty. This can help relax their sphincter muscles.

You can give your child some medication to soften their stool. Ask your GP if you think your child might need it. A change in diet to include more soluble fibre, extra fluid intake, validating their fears and a good sitting position makes a big difference alongside medication. Parents are often scared of using medication. My experience is that if it is used carefully, it can be extremely helpful to establish good habits and to make sure there is absolutely no pain for your child in passing the poo.

CONSTIPATION

Food travels through the body and ends up in the large intestine. A lack of fluids, lack of fibre, poor diet or excess sweating can cause the poo to remain in the large intestine or bowel too long. As a result of this, it dries out and constipation occurs. When you understand the physical process, you can explain it to your child. When their poo dries out, they haven't drunk enough, or their diet hasn't been good enough. You can actually show them what dried out mud looks like when it hasn't had enough water. **See Mud Experiment.**

Children will often need much more water than we realise, by the time they tell you they are thirsty they are already dehydrated so it is important to give the fluids really regularly. So the best way to help constipation is to make sure they have lots of fluids and water-rich foods. You can also make adjustments to their diet, adding in more soluble fibre (found in vegetables and fruit, beans, lentils, sweet potatoes and oats) Wheat fibre (found in is much less soluble) and wheat products made with white flour - such as pasta, biscuits and white bread have very little or no fibre at all. Kids also need lots of good fats found in nuts, avocado, oily fish, olive oil or coconut oil. That helps keep everything well-lubricated.

Problem-solve with Your Child

"How do you think we can get this problem sorted?". Very often they've got really good ideas. The aim is that you're collaborating, not pushing them. **"You find it hard to push your poo out because you're worried it's going to be painful. That's why we give you special medicine and lots of water. Also that's why we want you to sit regularly on the potty so you can make sure your muscles push the poo out. What else might help?".**

It's really important that you make the distinction that their body hasn't been working efficiently and their brain has given them the wrong instruction. The brain has given them the instruction to hold the poo in because it knows that it has been painful in the past and the body is holding the poo back. There's that separation, they know you're not blaming them. Discuss the feeling of relief when the poo passes. Some parents have videoed their child on the potty so that they can show their child the difference in how they feel before and after.

Watch Out for Patterns

There will be certain things that trigger bad patches,so as parents we need to be aware of what the triggers could be and prepare kids well in advance for changes or potentially stressful adverse events. Give your child lots of warning for things they're not going to like doing. Something that could trigger a bad patch of withholding might be that you have to go away and they have to stay with a relative overnight or with a babysitter. Other triggers might be a new school, going on holiday or a change in childcare. Prepare them well in advance for those sorts of things, rather than springing things on them. Preparing children in advance is a really good general parenting tool, as it helps children be emotionally ready for those changes.

Conclusion:

You've reached the conclusion of the book. Hopefully once you've successfully potty trained or are all-set to get started. If you do have regression, or if you want to refresh on descriptive praise and reflective listening, I hope you'll return to this book for a recap of these techniques.

I want to say thank you for reading this book. If you haven't started potty training yet, be sure that both you and your child are prepared for the transition into potty training. Preparation and communication are the key. That's the key for so many issues that you have with your children, to help prepare them for any changes. You want teenagers who will communicate with you, and tell you what they're afraid of and tell you if they're worried about things in their life. You want your children to feel proud of themselves and to speak out if they experience injustice. Good communication as a parent is absolutely vital and I hope you've picked up some ways to improve your communication with your child.

Remember to avoid comparisons: "My friend's child is the same age as mine and she was potty trained in two days!". If your child has been slow to adapt to potty training, don't force it. It is a very personal thing to do with your child and also your situation.

Don't forget to use descriptive praise, reflective listening all the time. Use it to describe things that you love about your child and for things that they're learning to do. Use descriptive praise and validate their emotions with reflective listening for absolutely everything, they are so invaluable to you for parenting from now and forever.

Try not to get too stressed about it. The less stressed you are about anything to do with raising children, the better the outcome is going to be. Remember, everyone gets there in the end. If you're using all the tools that I've given you in this book, you should get there successfully. It may take longer than you'd hoped, but you will get there. If you would like personal help from me, go to my website and we can set up a time to have a Discovery call. **www.myparentingsolutions.com.**

Camilla McGill, London, 2022

DOWNLOAD RESOURCES

Scan this QR code to take you directly to the special page on my website where you can get a free download of some great resources that I refer to in the book.

- **Stop and Go signs to show children**
- **The My Parenting Solutions child-friendly anatomical diagram**
- **A booklet of resources of child-friendly potty training books, apps and songs**